Clean Eating Cookbook 2021

50 natural and healthy recipes

Table of Contents

DAAL WITH PEAS AND ALMOND SEEDS PEA
SOUP WITH MINT AND PUMPERNICKEL
RED BEET SANDWICH WITH FRESH GOAT CHEESE
CLUB SANDWICH WITH CHICKEN AND ESTRAGON
MAYO PORTOBELLO BURGER WITH HONEY ONIONS
MINI FRIED TATAS WITH SPINACH AND SALMON
GUACAMOLE SANDWICH WITH TOMATO SALSA
"FISH & CHIPS" WITH SWEET POTATOES VEGGIE
FRICADEL WITH MOUNTAIN CHEESE WRAPS WITH
COD AND PEA CREAM
PULLED LAX BURGER WITH HORSE RADISH YOGURT
ROASTED VEGETABLE SANDWICH WITH CAPER PESTO
SPINACH WAFFLES WITH YOGURT AND CRESS PUTELLO
TONNATO SANDWICH WITH TURKEY BREAST VEGGIE
SLOPPY JOE WITH MOUNTAIN LENS AND CUCUMBER
COLESLAW BURGER WITH PECAN NUT AND FETA
SWEET PUMPKIN SANDWICH WITH PEANUT
JUTS FRENCH TOAST WITH CHUTNEY AND
AVOCADO WHOLE GRAIN BUTTER SPELLED
TOAST BREAD RYE BUTTERMILK BUNS
BENTO WITH NUT BREAD AND PEANUT JUTS TACO-BENTO
WITH CHILI CHICKEN AND GUACAMOLE SUMMERROLLS
BENTO WITH MANGO CUCUMBER SALAD FALAFEL-BENTO
WITH HUMMUS AND SALAD SATÉ-BENTO WITH CURRY
SAUCE AND NATURAL RICE SALAD ANTIPASTI-BENTO
WITH QUINOA SALAD AND OLIVES VEGETABLE BOX WITH
SHEEP CHEESE QUARK FRUIT BOX WITH MATCHA
YOGURT AND BASIL
SPICY VEGETABLE CHIPS WITH SESAME AND
ROSEMARY CURRY POPCORN WITH HONEY AND SEA
SALT CHERRY POWERBALLS WITH COCOA NIBS
NUT POWER BAR WITH HONEY AND CHIA SEEDS
WAFFLES WITH BLUEBERRIES AND COCOA NIBS

LIFESTYLE & NUTRITION

WHERE ARE WE TODAY?

As far as our diet is concerned, a lot has changed over the past 40 years. We have become more comfortable because we supposedly don't have the time to shop and cook. And the food producers and supermarkets have reacted to this. A curious look at the food supply shows that processed foods are flooding our grocery stores. The deep-freeze departments have become larger and offer us an unprecedented variety of low-nutrient, but high-calorie foods. Heavily processed foods contain innumerable approved food additives whose effects on the human organism have never been researched. And artificial flavor enhancers and aromas from the test tube ensure the taste. The food industry says it is safe in small quantities. This is doubtful when a person weighing 80 kilograms consumes around 75 tons of food in their lifetime.

When it comes to food choices, those that are "quick to prepare and inexpensive" are especially attractive. In advertising, the food industry leads us to believe that products are healthy and inexpensive. Those who let themselves be seduced by advertising slogans usually turn to products that no longer deserve the name "food". Among other things, these are responsible for the global obesity epidemic and the diseases of civilization that result from it. A person who weighs too much moves less in everyday life. An unstoppable vicious circle of little movement and increasing body weight begins.

THE ROUTE IS THE GOAL

You can only stop this development by changing your diet and lifestyle. Admittedly, habits that have been cultivated for years cannot be changed in a few days and it takes a certain amount of time to get rid of them. But with a little discipline and willpower, you can change eating habits in the long run that make you sick, sluggish and lackluster. The great thing about it is that you already have the capacity for discipline and willpower within you. All you have to do is press the correct "buttons" to activate them. If you choose to replace old habits with new ones, you will most certainly be rewarded for your ambition and perseverance. It maybe not today or tomorrow, but definitely at a later date. See each new day as an opportunity to make correct food choices and food preparation decisions. It's like a kind of health account into which you keep paying a small amount. This path will eventually give you the level of health and well-being that you have always wanted.

The way there is so easy! Avoid processed, refined and denatured foods and replace them with fresh, natural and naturally produced products, as propagated by the philosophy of clean eating. Clean eating is not necessarily vegan or vegetarian. However, this nutritional concept is the basis for all other forms of nutrition that we encounter in everyday life. Just start the changes today, stay tuned and find your new way!

WHAT IS CLEAN EATING?

In the broadest sense, clean eating means that food should be selected and consumed "clean", that is, as natural and unprocessed as possible.

But what do you mean by natural and unprocessed? Natural and unprocessed foods are all those that were not manufactured through an industrial process and that can be purchased in their original form as a product. You could also say quite banally: Do not buy products that are advertised, or: The shorter the list of ingredients, the better.

AS NATURAL AS POSSIBLE

The more processing steps a product has, the lower the content of vitamins and minerals. But this is exactly what the body needs, along with others, every day in order to be healthy and productive, as they support many functions in the body.

A lack of nutrients is usually associated with a higher calorie intake. This means that your body compensates for this lack of nutrients by increasing your appetite and constantly demands more food. It signals this to you through cravings and cravings for sweet or fatty foods. If you give in to the signals and satisfy this greed, then obesity is inevitable.

The ratio of calorie to nutrient content is an important point if you want to get rid of excess body fat easily and playfully or if you want to maintain your weight. Sure, the calorie balance is primarily decisive for weight gain or loss. The Clean Eating nutritional concept works without counting calories. After all, who wants to constantly pay attention to the calorie content of food in everyday life? Even if you just want to consciously enjoy and feel good all round, clean eating is a good choice, because the concept also has to offer that. This form of nutrition is always based on naturally grown foods, regardless of what you intend to do with the diet and what goals you are pursuing with it.

Well taken care of

Eating according to the clean-eating principle is the healthiest way to eat a balanced and wholesome diet. If you adjust your diet accordingly, you will get all of the essential nutrients your body needs to function reliably.

Another important cornerstone of clean eating is the balance between the fatty acids. Therefore, you should consume foods with both saturated and unsaturated fats.

In addition to healthy fatty acids, the clean-eating philosophy also includes the supply of sufficient proteins from plant and animal foods as a building material for your muscles. Because they are the engine of your metabolism. Finally, the body needs complex carbohydrates from whole grains, lettuce and vegetables. And because all processes in the body require water, regular drinking throughout the day is so important - preferably water or herbal tea.

WHAT ELSE IS IMPORTANT

It goes without saying that we want natural foods without chemical additives and should be normal for everyone. If you get natural, seasonal ingredients for your food at the farmer's market, organic or farm shop, that's a step in the right direction. Clean eaters buy fresh food and cook for themselves.

The concept provides for 4–5 meals spread over the day. Maybe that sounds strange at first and after a huge investment of time. But this is by no means the case in reality and can be easily managed with a little skill and good organization. In addition, the meals do not necessarily have to be elaborately cooked dishes. It can also be just a handful of nuts or raw vegetables.

Ideally, there should be 2–3 larger meals and 2 small snacks in between. Breakfast to start the day and a second larger meal, either at noon or in the evening, are essential pillars of the clean-eating philosophy, depending on the daily routine. However, the preparation of the meals takes some time. Snacks do not require a lot of time and, like the prepared main meals, can be taken anywhere in suitable packaging.

In order to supply the body with nutrients in the morning, a natural and high-fiber breakfast is the basis for every day. Oat flakes with a little berry fruit, for example, provide vital nutrients and can be prepared in a variety of ways. The typical breakfast roll with jam or sausage, on the other hand, is high in calories with a low nutritional content and minimal health benefits.

The background to regular meals is that the nutrients they supply stimulate your metabolism and keep blood sugar levels at a constant level. This means that food cravings don't stand a chance and you feel full all day long.

CLEAN EATING IN EVERYDAY LIFE

How you implement the clean eating philosophy in everyday life throughout your life differs from person to person and depends on the life situation. Since the concept is very simple in principle, anyone who wants to change their diet can adapt it to their needs. It's best to start with the recipes in this book. There is sure to be something for every taste. And the more you try, the more routine you get and can shorten the already short preparation times even further.

To get started, I recommend choosing 5–6 recipes that you like and that taste so good after trying them out that you can eat them again and again without them becoming too monotonous for you in the long run. Later you can exchange tried and tested recipes for others or expand the range of dishes as you wish. Once you have gained experience with clean eating, you can also create your own favorite dishes with clean ingredients. Because clean eaters are more concerned with their own nutrition and take the greatest good, namely their health, into their own hands.

THE FIRST STEP - SHOP CLEAN

You can avoid mistakes when shopping by choosing the right foods. At the beginning of the switch to clean eating, shopping can take longer than usual and can be a bit time-consuming. After all, you have to reorient yourself and critically examine what has been tried and tested so far. You should therefore plan a little more time for shopping and, at least at the beginning, read carefully the labels and lists of ingredients on the packaging until you know which additives are contained in the products. At some point, you will know your way around and know which groceries should regularly end up in your shopping cart and which ones you better keep your hands off of in the future. In order not to be tempted in the first place, avoid the confectionery and chips department, as well as refined sugar, white flour and products made from it, fast food and ready meals. First and foremost, start the shopping tour in the fruit and vegetable department and fill your shopping cart there.

Frozen products are perfectly okay as long as they are pure original products without additives. If you have little time to cook, a small supply of frozen vegetables is very useful. If necessary, it can be prepared quickly without thawing. The time required for this is minimal, and everyone has these few minutes left in the evening to prepare something healthy for dinner or for the next day.

If you prefer to buy canned or jared foods, choose foods that do not contain any preservatives, colorings, flavor enhancers, acidulants, or flavorings other than the main ingredient. Many industrially manufactured products also contain sugar. It is often disguised as dextrose, glucose syrup or maltodextrin. Pay attention to it the next time you shop! If you decide to go for cans or glasses every now and then, choose organic products whenever possible.

On the next page you will find a supply list with a small selection of clean foods that you should always have in the house.

BREAKFAST OR SNACK

Clean eaters have breakfast every day. Take enough time for breakfast and get up a little earlier if necessary. This will be easy for you after a while, because those who follow the clean eating philosophy are fit in the morning and start the day full of vigor. If you don't have time to have breakfast in the morning, take a snack with you on the go - a handful of nuts or a portion of fruit is always good. Or make yourself a smoothie. Anyone who claims they cannot eat in the morning is succumbing to their old habits. You can change this "bad" habit with a little discipline.

A handful of almonds with blueberries, quark mixed with flaxseed, Greek yogurt with your favorite berries and crushed flaxseed or two hard-boiled eggs with a handful of almonds are also suitable as a quick snack. A piece of fruit with almond butter would be another way of supplying the body with valuable nutrients in the morning.

THINK ABOUT TOMORROW IN THE EVENING

In the recipe section you will find lots of dishes that you can prepare well and safely packaged to take with you on the go. It's best to cook in the evening for the next day. Smart clean eaters prepare twice as much, eat one portion straight away and freeze the rest for the next few days.

And if you don't have the leisure to cook, that's not so bad. Then simply prepare fresh vegetables in bite-sized pieces, for example tomatoes, peppers, cucumbers, carrots or whatever else tastes good to you. With a homemade dip made from lean quark and freshly chopped herbs, the raw vegetables taste wonderful and are ideal for on the go.

STOCK LIST

OILS & FATS
Avocado oil
Coconut oil, native
Linseed oil, native
Extra virgin olive oil
Rapeseed oil
Walnut oil

NUTS & NUTS
Hazelnut kernels
Pumpkin seeds
Almonds
Pine nuts
Sunflower seeds
Walnut kernels

CARBOHYDRATE SOURCES
amaranth
Buckwheat
Spelled semolina
Green kernels
oatmeal
Brown rice
Quinoa

LEGUMES
Beans
Peas
Chickpeas
lenses

SPICES & HERBS
Chili flakes
ginger
Caraway seed
Turmeric powder
sea-salt
Ground cinnamon

basil
parsley
peppermint
chives
SUPERFOOD
Chia seeds
Cranberries
Goji berries
Hemp seeds, crushed
Cocoa nibs
Flaxseed, crushed
Matcha tea
MISCELLANEOUS
Organic almond butter
Organic peanut butter
Raisins, unsulphurized
Apple Cider Vinegar
White wine vinegar

ON THE GO

Anyone who takes their food with them to the office, school or university or simply wants to have a picnic in the countryside needs a suitable container or safe packaging for the self-cooked food. In summer you should also keep the prepared food refrigerated until you can enjoy it. The refrigerator in the office kitchen or cooling devices that you can connect to a cigarette lighter is ideal for this. But a cool box also works well on longer trips.

As a container and for packaging, there are different options, depending on what you want to take with you on the go or in between. The palette ranges from cling film and aluminum foil to sandwich or baking paper to freezer bags and lunch boxes, thermos cups or thermos flasks.

If you have plastic cans at home, make sure they are free from chemical softeners. Food-safe containers are marked with this symbol:

If you are buying new containers and want to be absolutely sure, opt for containers made of glass or other materials. You can buy them on the internet, in a homeware store, or in a well-stocked homeware corner in a department store. On these pages I will show you which these can be and what they are suitable for.

GLASS CONTAINER

For self-mixed smoothies and freshly squeezed juices, there are great glass bottles with screw caps that even have additional protective insulation. This protects against

Broken glass and insulates cold or warm contents. Glass offers many advantages over plastic and there are several arguments in favor of glass:

1. There are no chemical reactions and therefore no substances can pass into the food.

2. Glass is tasteless and odorless and therefore does not change the taste of the food.

3. Glass is more hygienic and easier to clean. Plastic containers can take on the colors or smells of the stored food after a short time.

4. Due to the thermal conductivity, the cooling is much more efficient than with plastic containers. This means that the food stays fresh longer.

5. Glass is durable for a lifetime and does not leave any waste behind.

6. Glass is dishwasher and microwave safe.

One disadvantage, however, could be that glass is heavier than any other material. For the problem that glass containers for food are difficult to close, there is a solution with a plastic lid. There is no contact with the food and the lid can be removed for heating. For me this is the optimal solution.

You can transport cold things such as dips and salad dressings or soups and small snacks for in between, for example, in a simple mason jar or a clean screw-top jar. So-called "Mason Jars", the stylish preserving jars from the USA, are closed with a metal lid with a plastic coating on the inside. Again, there is usually no contact with the food and the jar is sealed airtight.

BENTOBOXES

The idea of dividing a food container into small compartments originally came from Japan and has a long tradition there. The great clarity and the easy portioning of the food make the Bento box the ideal everyday companion for clean eaters. You can put several small meals in the box and take them with you wherever you go. Bento boxes are also available in different materials, colors and sizes, with and without cutlery.

STAINLESS STEEL

One of my favorites is the stylish bento box made of stainless steel, which is available in all possible sizes. As with glass, the advantages are hygiene, odorless ness and chemical inactivity.

Stainless steel has been used in large food companies for a long time and, happily, is now also conquering the market for domestic use. The advantage over glass is its lighter weight. The disadvantage is a possible leak. Because a stainless steel box without a rubber seal is not 100 percent airtight, so you should not transport liquid food in it. It is also important to mention that stainless steel containers must never be placed in the microwave.

WOOD

There are also containers made of wood that are suitable for transporting food. Wood insulates well and is light as a feather. Often it is cedar wood, the surface of which has been treated with a natural and food-safe varnish. I've also seen boxes made of ash wood that were turned from one piece. These have been oiled ecologically and even withstand moisture. Wooden boxes are generally unsuitable for the dishwasher and microwave.

THE AGONY OF CHOICE

Which box is suitable for which purpose always depends on the food that is to be transported in it. It is also important to note whether you want to spoon straight out of the box or eat from a plate. Other helpful considerations are whether you want to clean the container in the dishwasher and put the box in a microwave to warm up the meal. If you are clear about this, you are sure to make the right choice.

THE MUNTERMAKER - DAILY SMOOTHIES
INGREDIENTS:

Red smoothie:

100 g beetroot

250 g raspberries, frozen

1 banana

1 apple

1 teaspoon grated

ginger ½ pomegranate

2 teaspoons chia seeds

300 ml coconut water

1 lemon

Yellow smoothie:

1 mango

1 apple

1 banana

1 orange

1 lemon

1 teaspoon turmeric

1 teaspoon of hemp seeds

300 ml coconut water

Green smoothie:

1 avocado

1 handful of spinach

1 banana

1 lime

1 pear
1 teaspoon chia seeds
8 mint leaves
500 ml almond milk
2 tbsp yogurt
2 PEOPLE

HOW TO DO IT:

Prepare the vegetables and fruit for the smoothies ready to cook, cut them into small pieces and finely puree all the ingredients together in a high-performance mixer.

Tips

The liquid - whether coconut water or almond milk - can vary according to taste. Depending on the sweetness of the fruit, you can also help with honey or agave syrup.

ACAI SMOOTHIE BOWL WITH COCONUT AND CINNAMON

INGREDIENTS:

For the acai smoothie:
2 bananas
1 tbsp chia seeds
200 g acai fruit puree
160 g mixed berries, frozen
300 ml coconut milk

½ lime
½ teaspoon cinnamon powder
1 tbsp honey
For the topping:
Quinoa Pops
Coconut flakes
Pumpkin seeds
Chia seeds
Cocoa nibs Berry
mix
2 PEOPLE

HOW TO DO IT:

1. Put the bananas cut into pieces and the chia seeds in a bartender (blender). Puree together with the acai fruit puree, the berry mix and the coconut milk.

2. Finally, just add a little lime juice, the cinnamon powder and a little honey to taste.

3. Pour the acai smoothie into a bowl and sprinkle with plenty of topping as you like before eating.

tip

Instead of coconut milk, you can also use a plant-based milk of your choice.

BIRCHER PORRIDGE WITH NUTS AND SEEDS

INGREDIENTS:

For the Bircher porridge:

100 g crispy oat flakes

1 tbsp flaxseed, crushed

1 tbsp hemp seeds, crushed

30 g pumpkin seeds

40 g hazelnut kernels

1 apple and pear each

1 organic lime

1 teaspoon cinnamon powder

½ teaspoon cardamom

1 pinch of nutmeg

1 pinch of salt

1–2 tbsp honey, to taste

300 ml almond milk, unsweetened

For the topping:

Fruit and berries

Pumpkin seeds

Hazelnut kernels

Cocoa nibs

2 PEOPLE

HOW TO DO IT:

1. Mix the crispy oat flakes with the flax seeds, hemp seeds and pumpkin seeds the day before. Chop roughly the hazelnuts and add.

2. Coarsely grate the apple and pear and marinate with the zest and juice of a lime. Add the rasps to the oat flakes, refine with the spices and season with a little honey. Finally, pour in the almond milk and let it steep in the refrigerator overnight.

3. Refine "on top" with fresh fruit and berries, pumpkin seeds, hazelnuts and cocoa nibs as desired.

Tips

A dollop of yoghurt "on top" makes the porridge even creamier. If you like, you can add a handful of cranberries or goji berries.

GRANOLA WITH FRUIT SALAD AND ALMOND CREAM

INGREDIENTS:

For the granola:

80 g of crispy oat flakes

40 g each of quinoa and almond sticks

20 g sunflower seeds

20 g pumpkin seeds

2 tbsp coconut oil or cocoa butter

60 g honey

1 teaspoon cinnamon powder

Nutmeg and salt

For the almond cream:

100 g almonds

60 g cashew nuts

200 ml almond milk

1 tbsp honey

½ vanilla pod

For the fruit salad:

Seasonal fruit and berries

Pomegranate seeds

1 organic lime

2 PEOPLE

HOW TO DO IT:

1. Preheat the oven to 160 ° C for the granola.

2. Mix the hearty oat flakes, quinoa, almond sticks, sunflower seeds and pumpkin seeds together.

3. Then melt the coconut oil and stir together with the honey, cinnamon powder and a pinch of nutmeg and salt each. Mix this marinade well with the oatmeal mixture. Spread the granola flat on a baking tray lined with baking paper and bake until golden yellow for about 30 minutes; turn every 10 minutes. Then let the granola cool down on the tray and crumble roughly.

4. Cover the almonds and cashew nuts with water and leave to soak for at least 4 hours. Then pour off the water and puree the nuts together with the almond milk, honey and the pulp of the vanilla pod to a smooth cream.

5. For the fruit salad, cut any fruit into bite-sized pieces and marinate with the zest and juice of the lime.

6. Layer the fruit salad with the almond cream and the granola, enjoy pure or add a little almond milk.

Tips

Instead of honey, you can also use maple syrup and sweeten it more or less depending on your taste. Here it is worthwhile to make more granola right away. When packed airtight, it can be kept for several weeks.

POWER MUFFINS WITH ALMONDS
AND CINNAMON

INGREDIENTS:

150 g wholemeal spelled flour
100 g almond semolina
120 g coconut blossom sugar or raw cane sugar
2 teaspoons of pure tartar baking powder
1 teaspoon cinnamon powder
3 eggs

60 g applesauce
80 g coconut oil
1 organic orange
1 carrot
1 apple
1 tbsp cranberries
1 tbsp sunflower seeds
1 tbsp pumpkin seeds
1 tbsp almond sticks
Approx. 10 MUFFINS

HOW TO DO IT:

1. Firstly, mix the whole wheat flour with almond semolina, coconut blossom sugar, baking powder and cinnamon.

2. Whisk the eggs, add applesauce and melted coconut oil, then stir in the zest and juice of the orange. Then mix everything together well with the flour without lumps.

3. Peel the carrot and grate it roughly like the apple. Mix together with the cranberries, sunflower seeds, pumpkin seeds and the almond sticks and fold into the batter.

4. Pour the dough into greased or paper-lined muffin tins and bake at 180 ° C for about 15–20 minutes until golden. Then let it cool down for 5 minutes. An ideal breakfast for on the go!

tip

The power muffins stay fresh for several days at room temperature and sealed airtight.

FRUITY PUMPKIN SOUP WITH CURRY AND COCONUT

INGREDIENTS:

250 g pumpkin, e.g. B. Hokkaido
1 onion
1 clove of garlic
1 tbsp coconut oil
1 tbsp red curry paste, more or less depending
on your taste 200 ml vegetable stock
200 ml coconut milk
1 star anise
½ cinnamon stick

1 bay leaf
1 organic orange
Salt pepper
To serve:
virgin pumpkin seed oil
Chia seeds
puffed amaranth
some chervil
2 PEOPLE

HOW TO DO IT:

1. Halve, core and roughly dice the pumpkin. Peel and dice finely the onion and garlic. Simmer together in the coconut oil until translucent. Then add the curry paste and roast with it.

2. Deglaze with the vegetable stock and coconut milk, add the spices and cook for 20 minutes until soft. Then remove the spices again and puree the soup finely. Refine with the zest and juice of the orange and season with a little salt and pepper.

3. To serve, drizzle with a little pumpkin seed oil, sprinkle with chia seeds, puffed amaranth and plucked chervil.

Tips

The Hokkaido is the only pumpkin that doesn't have to be peeled. If you don't like orange, you can replace it with a dash of naturally cloudy apple juice.

FRESH SUMMER SOUP WITH KEFIR AND DILL

INGREDIENTS:
2 eggs
300 g potatoes, waxy
200 g cucumber
200 g radishes, without greens
4 stalks of spring onions
1 handful of fresh dill
2 tbsp olive oil

1 lime
1 teaspoon coarse organic
mustard Salt pepper
To serve:
350 ml kefir
150 ml of mineral water
2 PEOPLE

HOW TO DO IT:

1. First, boil the eggs for 9 minutes and cook the potatoes in salted water for about 20 minutes. Then let cool and cut into slices.

2. In the meantime, cut the cucumber, radishes and spring onions into fine slices.

3. Chop finely the dill and mix with the olive oil, the juice of the lime and the mustard. Season well with salt and pepper.

4. Mix everything and pour into glasses.

5. Mix the kefir with the sparkling mineral water and pour it over the vegetables before serving.

tip

The vegetables can be added or exchanged as an insert. Just try a few combinations!

AVOCADO FENNEL SALAD WITH GRAPEFRUIT

INGREDIENTS:

For the salad:

1 avocado

½ cucumber

200 g cherry tomatoes

2 small fennel

bulbs ½ red onion

1 handful of rocket

1 handful of coriander greens or parsley
For the dressing:
1 pink grapefruit
6 tbsp olive oil
2 teaspoons of honey
1 organic lime
1 handful of mint
2 PEOPLE

HOW TO DO IT:

1. Halve the avocado, core it and remove it from the skin. Cut the pulp together with the cucumber into small cubes. Halve the cherry tomatoes.

2. Slice finely the fennel and the red onion. Mix everything with the rocket and finely plucked coriander greens or parsley.

3. For the dressing, peel and fillet the pink grapefruit with a knife, collecting the juice. Cut the fillets into small pieces and add to the salad. Mix the grapefruit juice with the olive oil, the honey and a little zest and juice of the lime well. Add finely chopped mint and season with salt and pepper.

4. Marinate the salad fresh with the dressing and enjoy.

Tips

The salad becomes even fruity with a finely grated apple. If you like, you can replace the pink grapefruit with an orange.

QUINOA SALAD WITH OLIVES AND FETA

INGREDIENTS:

For the quinoa salad:

100 g quinoa

2 tomatoes

1 red pepper

1 red onion

½ cucumber

1 handful of olives, sliced

100 g feta cheese

1 handful of parsley

For the dressing:

6 tbsp olive oil

1 organic lemon

1 teaspoon honey

1 clove of garlic

Salt pepper

2 PEOPLE

HOW TO DO IT:

1. Rinse the quinoa with cold water and cook in 200 ml of water over a low heat for about 15 minutes. Then let it cool down.

2. In the meantime, quarter and core the tomatoes. Halve the peppers and remove the seeds. Peel the onion and cut everything together - as well as the cucumber - into fine cubes. Finally, mix the vegetables with the quinoa and olives. Crumble the feta and mix with the salad together with finely chopped parsley.

3. For the dressing, mix the olive oil with the zest and juice of the lemon and honey. Peel the garlic clove and chop it very finely, add to the dressing and season with salt and pepper.

4. Marinate the salad with the dressing and enjoy.

Tips

If you like, you can fold in a few more peppers. Depending on the season, the salad can also be complemented well with asparagus or pumpkin.

CAPRESE BREAD SALAD WITH PESTO AND RUCOLA

INGREDIENTS:

For the Caprese bread salad:
3–4 slices of wholemeal bread, e.g. B. Nut-spelled bread from p. 96 (see also tip p. 39)
2 tbsp olive oil

125 g mini mozzarella

250 g cherry tomatoes

1 handful of rocket

For the basil pesto:

30 g basil

1 tbsp pine nuts, toasted

1 clove of garlic

80-100 ml of olive oil

½ organic lemon

20 g parmesan cheese

Salt pepper

2 PEOPLE

HOW TO DO IT:

1. At the beginning, cut the whole wheat bread into small cubes, place on a tray and drizzle with the olive oil. Bake in the oven at 180 ° C (200 ° C top / bottom heat) until crispy for 5–10 minutes, then leave to cool.

2. In the meantime, finely puree the basil, pine nuts, peeled garlic clove, olive oil and lemon juice. Finally, refine with finely grated parmesan and season with salt and pepper.

3. For the salad, drain the mini mozzarella and put it in a glass with the pesto. Put the quartered cherry tomatoes on top, then add the rocket and top with the toasted bread cubes.

4. Shake the glass vigorously or stir well before eating.

tip

Ask your trusted baker for the bread's ingredients list. It should always be made from whole grain flour and free from refined sugar and additives. Some bakeries and supermarkets have bread with raw cane sugar or honey in their range.

SOBA SALAD WITH ASPARAGUS AND OYSTER MUSHROOMS

ingredients:

For the soba salad:
100 g soba noodles
1 red onion and 1 clove of garlic each
150 g green asparagus
120 g oyster mushrooms
1 carrot and 1 pepper each
2 stalks of spring onions

2 tbsp coconut oil
1 tbsp sesame seeds
Thai basil and coriander leaves
Salt pepper
For the dressing:
½ chili pepper
1 teaspoon ginger zest
3 tbsp tamari soy sauce
1 organic lime
6 tbsp sesame oil
1 teaspoon maple syrup
1 tbsp fish sauce, optional
2 PEOPLE

HOW TO DO IT:

1. At the beginning, boil the soba noodles in plenty of salted water for 4–5 minutes, drain and rinse in cold water.

2. Peel the onion and garlic and cut into fine strips. Cut off the woody ends of the asparagus and cut into bite-sized pieces together with the oyster mushrooms. Peel the carrot and cut into fine strips. Cut the pepper and spring onion into fine slices.

3. Sear the oyster mushrooms in the coconut oil. Add onion, garlic and pepper. Then stir in the asparagus and carrot and fry for 5 minutes over a low heat. Then remove the vegetables from the stove, season with salt and pepper and let cool down a little.

4. Prepare the dressing. To do this, chop the chili pepper and mix well with the remaining ingredients.

5. Finally, mix the soba noodles with the vegetables, marinate with the dressing and refine with a little sesame and freshly picked herbs.

tip

Make sure that the soba noodles are made from 100% buckwheat.

MISO SOUP WITH VEGETABLES AND SESAME

INGREDIENTS:

For the miso soup:
2 tbsp red miso paste (Hatcho Miso)
1 organic lime
2 tbsp tamari soy sauce
2 teaspoons sesame oil
½ chili pepper

2 tsp ginger zest

½ teaspoon salt

For the deposit:

½ red onion and ½ red bell pepper each

1 stalk of celery

¼ Chinese cabbage, 1 small

carrot 50 g sugar snap peas

50 g shiitake mushrooms

2 stalks of spring onions

30 g whole grain rice noodles

Miscellaneous:

1 tablespoon each of sesame seeds and cashew nuts

1 handful of Thai basil

2 PEOPLE

HOW TO DO IT:

1. At the beginning mix the red miso paste with the juice of the lime, the soy sauce, sesame oil, finely chopped chili, the ginger zest and the salt. Put the cream in a heat-resistant glass.

2. For the insert, cut the onion into fine strips. Clean, wash and core the vegetables and cut everything into very fine strips. Cut the mushrooms and spring onions into thin slices. Layer everything together with the wholemeal rice noodles in the glass.

3. Finally, sprinkle with some sesame, cashew nuts and fresh Thai basil.

4. To prepare, pour 300–400 ml of boiling water over it and let it steep for 5–8 minutes, stirring occasionally.

tip

The soup can be varied as you like, but you should pay attention to short preparation times.

VEGETABLE SALAD WITH MUSTARD DRESSING AND EGG

INGREDIENTS:

For the vegetable salad:
300 g small potatoes
1 teaspoon caraway seeds
200 g carrots
100 g broccoli
100 g celery
1 red onion

3 sticks of spring onions

1 handful of parsley

For the mustard dressing:

5 tbsp olive oil

2 tbsp apple cider vinegar

½ organic orange

2 teaspoons of organic mustard

1 teaspoon honey

Miscellaneous:

2 eggs Salt

pepper

2 PEOPLE

HOW TO DO IT:

1. At the beginning, cook the potatoes in plenty of salted water with the caraway seeds for about 20 minutes. Drain, let cool down and cut in half or quarter, depending on the size.

2. In the meantime, wash the vegetables, peel the carrot and onion and cut everything into bite-sized pieces. Place salted water in a saucepan and gradually blanch the vegetables until they are al dente.

3. Then mix the vegetables with the finely chopped spring onions, chopped parsley and the potatoes.

4. For the dressing, mix the olive oil with the apple cider vinegar, a little zest and juice of the orange, mustard and honey and season well with salt and pepper.

5. Marinate the vegetable salad with the mustard dressing and let it steep for about 15 minutes.

6. Finally, cook the eggs in simmering water for 5–6 minutes until they are waxy, remove them and let them cool down. Then peel and serve with the vegetable salad.

tip

The vegetables can of course be varied depending on the season and taste.

GAZPACHO WITH CHILI AND GOJI BERRIES

INGREDIENTS:

For the gazpacho:

200 g red pepper

1 onion

1 clove of garlic

450 g ripe tomatoes on the vine

250 g cucumber

½-1 chili pepper

½ teaspoon paprika powder, noble sweet

2 tbsp olive oil

1 tbsp red wine vinegar

1 organic lime

Miscellaneous:

1 stalk of celery

1/3 cucumber

2 tbsp goji berries

1 handful of basil

and Coriander

green Salt pepper

2 PEOPLE

HOW TO DO IT:

1. For the gazpacho, halve and core the red pepper. Peel and chop roughly the onion and garlic. Puree everything very finely together with tomatoes, cucumber, chili pepper, paprika powder, olive oil and red wine vinegar. Season to taste with the zest and juice of a lime, salt and pepper.

2. Then pass everything through a sieve and refrigerate the gazpacho for at least 30 minutes.

3. In the meantime, cut the celery and the cucumber into fine cubes. Mix with the goji berries and finely chopped herbs and use as a filler.

tip

If you like it even more fruity, you can also puree half a tuber of fennel or 1 handful of strawberries.

VEGETABLE CURRY WITH COCONUT AND CASHEW SEEDS

INGREDIENTS:

For the curry paste:

2 shallots and 2 cloves of garlic each

1 handful each of coriander greens
and Thai basil
1-2 chili peppers
1 stick of lemongrass
2 kaffir lime leaves
1 walnut-sized piece of ginger
1 organic lime
For the vegetable curry:
200 g shiitake mushrooms
100 g green beans
100 g sugar snap peas
2 tbsp coconut oil
200 ml vegetable stock or water
300 ml coconut milk
1 handful of cashew nuts, toasted
1 handful of Thai basil and coriander
greens Salt pepper
2 PEOPLE

HOW TO DO IT:

1. Firstly, make the curry paste. Peel the shallots and the garlic. Puree as finely as possible in a high-performance mixer together with coriander, Thai basil, chili peppers, finely chopped lemongrass, kaffir lime leaves, finely grated ginger as well as zest and juice of the lime.

2. Cut the shiitake mushrooms, green beans and snow peas into bite-sized pieces. Sear the mushrooms in the coconut oil and add the vegetable stock and coconut milk. Simmer over a low heat for about 5 minutes, then add the beans and let everything simmer gently for another 5 minutes.

3. Finally, add the snow peas and curry paste, bring to the boil and season with salt and pepper.

4. Refine the curry with roasted cashew nuts and freshly chopped Thai basil and coriander leaves.

tip

If you like, you can replace or add to the vegetables. Also delicious with chicken; Add the chicken breast cut into cubes 5 minutes before the end of the cooking time.

ZUCCHINI SALAD WITH NUTS AND FETA CHEESE

INGREDIENTS:

For the zucchini salad:
300 g zucchini, green and yellow

3 tbsp hazelnut kernels
3 tbsp hazelnut oil
1 organic orange
1 teaspoon honey
1 pinch of cayenne pepper
Salt pepper
Miscellaneous:
100 g feta cheese
1 handful of mint
2 PEOPLE

HOW TO DO IT:

1. Wash the zucchini and cut off the ends. Use a spiral cutter to cut the zucchini into spaghetti.

2. Roast the hazelnuts in a pan without oil and let them cool, then roughly chop and mix with the zucchini.

3. Mix the salad with the hazelnut oil, a little zest and juice from the orange and the honey. Season to taste with a pinch of cayenne pepper, salt and pepper.

4. Crumble finely the feta and add to the salad with finely chopped mint just before eating.

tip

If you don't like hazelnuts or have an allergic reaction, you can also use olive.

MANGO PAPAYA SALAD WITH PRAWNS

INGREDIENTS:

For the salad:

400 g of ripe papaya
½ mango
150 g cherry tomatoes
1 red onion
1 head of romaine lettuce
1 handful of coriander greens or parsley
6 red shell prawns
½ organic lime
1 tbsp olive oil
Salt pepper

For the dressing:

2 tbsp papaya seeds
with something Pulp
3 tbsp olive oil
1 organic lime
1 teaspoon each of honey and fish sauce
½ pepper
2 PEOPLE

HOW TO DO IT:

1. Firstly, halve, core and peel the papaya. Keep 2 tablespoons of seeds for the dressing. Cut the pulp into even cubes.

2. Peel the mango, remove the stone and dice the pulp. Halve the cherry tomatoes and cut the red onion into fine strips. Pluck the romaine lettuce into bite-sized pieces and mix all ingredients with finely chopped coriander leaves.

3. For the dressing, puree finely the papaya seeds with the olive oil, a little zest and the juice of a lime as well as the honey, the fish sauce and the pepper. Finally, season with salt and pepper and marinate the salad with it.

4. Remove the prawns from the shell and carefully remove the intestines

using a small knife. Fry in a little olive oil for about 2 minutes per side and season with a little salt and a splash of lime juice.

5. Put the salad in the glass and the prawns "on top".

DAAL WITH PEAS AND ALMOND SEEDS

INGREDIENTS:

For the Daal:

1 onion
1 clove of garlic
1 chili pepper

100 g tomatoes
½ tbsp mustard seeds
1 teaspoon cumin
2 tbsp coconut oil
1 teaspoon turmeric
200 g red lentils
300 ml coconut milk
100 g peas, frozen
1 teaspoon fresh ginger
1 organic lime
Salt pepper

Miscellaneous:

1 handful of coriander greens
1 handful of almond kernels, toasted
2 PEOPLE

HOW TO DO IT:

1. Firstly, dice the peeled onion and garlic clove as well as the chili pepper. Dice roughly the tomatoes and set aside. Crush the mustard seeds and cumin in a mortar.

2. Sauté the onion cubes with the garlic and the crushed spices in the coconut oil until translucent. Add the turmeric and lentils, toast briefly and add the diced tomatoes. Pour 300 ml of water and coconut milk on top and cook on a low heat for about 25 minutes until smooth.

3. Then add the peas and simmer for another 5 minutes. Refine with freshly grated ginger, zest and juice of the lime and season with salt and pepper.

4. Sprinkle with chopped coriander greens and roasted almond kernels before serving.

tip

If you like, you can refine "on top" with Greek yoghurt.

PEA SOUP WITH MINT AND PUMPERNICKEL

INGREDIENTS:

For the pea soup:

3 shallots

1 clove of garlic

1 tbsp olive oil

1 teaspoon whole cane sugar

1 pinch of cumin

500 ml vegetable stock or water

250 g peas, frozen

1 handful of mint
½ organic
lime nutmeg
Salt pepper
Miscellaneous:
pumpernickel
Spring leek mint

2 PEOPLE

HOW TO DO IT:

1. Peel the shallots and the clove of garlic, cut into small pieces and sauté in the olive oil with the whole cane sugar and a pinch of cumin until translucent. Top up with the vegetable stock and bring to the boil briefly.

2. Then add the peas and mint and simmer for 5 minutes over low heat. Puree everything together very finely, strain the soup through a fine sieve and season with a little lime juice, freshly grated nutmeg, salt and pepper.

3. As an insert, cut the pumpernickel into fine cubes, the spring onions into fine rings and the mint into fine strips. Add the filler just before eating.

RED BEET SANDWICH WITH FRESH GOAT CHEESE

INGREDIENTS:

For the beetroot sandwich:

250 g beetroot

1 apple

1 tbsp extra virgin olive oil

2 sprigs of thyme

1 teaspoon honey

4 slices of wholemeal bread, e.g. B. Nut-spelled bread from p. 96 (see also tip p. 39)

50 g goat cream cheese

endive salad

Garden cress

Salt pepper

For the vegetable sticks:

1 carrot

½ cucumber

1 bell pepper

2 PEOPLE

HOW TO DO IT:

1. At the beginning, peel the beetroot and wrap it in aluminum foil and bake it in the oven at 200 ° C for about 60 minutes until soft, then let it cool down and slice it into thin slices.

2. Quarter and core the apple and cut into thin wedges. Fry briefly in the olive oil and refine with thyme and honey.

3. Toast the wholemeal bread on both sides and brush with the goat's cream cheese. Cover with beetroot slices and pour a pinch of salt and a little pepper over them. Finally, add the apple wedges and finish with endive salad, a little garden cress and the toasted wholemeal bread.

4. Cut the vegetables for the sticks into finger-thick strips and serve with the beetroot sandwich.

tip

It is best to bake a few more beets in the same batch. These can be kept in the refrigerator for 1 week and can be processed into a cream or salad.

CLUB SANDWICH WITH CHICKEN AND

ESTRAGON MAYO

INGREDIENTS:

For the chicken breast:
2 chicken breasts
½ teaspoon paprika powder
1 tbsp olive oil
For the tarragon
mayo: 80 ml soy milk
½ lemon
1 teaspoon organic mustard
1 handful of tarragon
150 ml rapeseed oil
50 g crème fraîche
Miscellaneous:
6 slices of wholemeal butter spelled toast (see p. 92)
1 avocado
2 hard-boiled eggs
1 tomato and 1 red onion each
Romaine lettuce
Salt pepper
2 PEOPLE

HOW TO DO IT:

1. Season the chicken breasts with salt, pepper and paprika powder. Fry in the olive oil over medium heat for 5–7 minutes on each side. Let rest briefly and cut into slices.

2. For the mayo, mix the soy milk with the lemon juice and mustard. Puree with the hand blender together with the tarragon and add gradually small amounts of oil until you have a mayonnaise. Refine with the crème fraîche and season with salt and pepper.

3. For the club sandwich, toast the wholemeal toasted bread until golden. Slice the avocado, hard-boiled eggs, tomato and the red onion.

4. Brush the first floor with tarragon mayonnaise and top with some romaine lettuce, avocado and egg.

5. Coat the second floor with the mayo again, top with the onion, tomato slices and the chicken breast. Finish the sandwich with some romaine lettuce and wholemeal toast bread "on top".

Tips

The sandwich is even more delicate with crispy fried bacon. Vegetarians can substitute roasted peppers for the chicken.

PORTOBELLO BURGER WITH HONEY ONIONS

INGREDIENTS:

For the Portobello:

1 clove of garlic

1 sprig of rosemary

2 tbsp olive oil

Cayenne pepper

2 portobello mushrooms

For the fried onions:

1 large onion

1 apple

1 tbsp olive oil

1 tbsp cranberries

1 orange

2 tablespoons each of apple cider vinegar and honey

Miscellaneous:

2 whole wheat rolls

Organic mustard

Lettuce hearts

parsley

Salt pepper

2 PEOPLE

HOW TO DO IT:

1. Preheat the oven to 200 ° C circulating air (220 ° C top / bottom heat).

2. Peel and chop the clove of garlic. Also chop the rosemary and season with the olive oil, a pinch of cayenne pepper, a little salt and pepper. Marinate the cleaned portobello mushrooms with it and bake in the oven for about 15 minutes.

3. In the meantime, peel the onion and cut into fine slices like the apple. Roast them in olive oil over medium heat, then add the cranberries and

deglaze with the juice of the orange. Add the apple cider vinegar and honey and reduce to a low heat for about 5 minutes.

4. For the portobello burger, roast the whole grain rolls on the cut surfaces and brush with a little mustard. Place a few leaves from the lettuce heart and the portobello mushroom on top and finish with freshly plucked parsley and rolls.

MINI FRIED TATAS WITH SPINACH AND SALMON

INGREDIENTS:

4 eggs
2 Table spoons of milk
Salt pepper
nutmeg
200 g salmon fillet, boned and skinless
1 tbsp butter
125 g baby spinach
6 MUFFINS

HOW TO DO IT:

1. Preheat the oven to 160 ° C circulating air (180 ° C top / bottom heat).

2. Whisk the eggs with the milk and season well with salt, pepper and freshly grated nutmeg.

3. Rinse the salmon fillet with cold water, pat dry and cut into small cubes. Grease a muffin tin with butter. Spread the baby spinach together with the salmon cubes in the molds. Fill the muffin tin evenly with the whisked egg.

4. Then put the frittatas in the oven for about 15 minutes and let them cool down slightly. Serve in paper cases.

tip

If you like it spicier, you can add a handful of grated Parmesan before baking.

GUACAMOLE SANDWICH WITH TOMATO SALSA

INGREDIENTS:

For the guacamole:
2 avocados
1 lime
2 tbsp olive oil
1 clove of garlic
½ – 1 chili pepper, depending
on Sharpness

1 tomato
For the tomato salsa:
200 g vine tomatoes
1/3 cucumber
½ red onion 2
 tbsp olive oil
½ lime
1 handful of fresh coriander
Miscellaneous:
Whole grain bread, e.g. B. Nut-
spelled bread Salt pepper
2 PEOPLE

HOW TO DO IT:

1. Halve the avocados, remove the stone, remove the pulp from the skin and dice. Marinate with the juice of a lime and the olive oil. Peel the garlic clove and chop it very finely together with the chili pepper and add to the avocados. Process into a puree with a fork. Then quarter and core the tomato and cut the tomato fillets into cubes. Fold the diced tomatoes into the guacamole and season with salt and pepper.

2. For the salsa, cut the tomatoes and cucumber into small cubes. Cut the onion into thin slices. Mix the olive oil with the lime juice to a dressing and season with salt and pepper. Marinate the salsa with it and refine it with freshly chopped coriander greens.

3. Brush the wholemeal bread with the guacamole as desired and top with the tomato salsa.

tip

The guacamole also tastes very good with the vegetable chips (see p. 114) and is an ideal companion at every celebration.

"FISH & CHIPS" WITH SWEET POTATOES

INGREDIENTS:

For the sweet potatoes:
2 sweet potatoes
1 tbsp cornstarch
½ teaspoon cayenne
pepper Salt pepper
4 tbsp coconut oil
For the saithe:
250 g pollack, boned and skinless

2 eggs

½ organic lime

2 teaspoons of curry powder

2 tbsp wholemeal spelled flour

2 tablespoons of oatmeal, tender as a flower Wholemeal spelled flour for turning Olive oil for frying

For the honey mustard sauce:

100 g crème fraîche

2 tbsp organic mustard, 1 tbsp honey

2 PEOPLE

HOW TO DO IT:

1. Preheat the oven to 200 ° C (220 ° C top / bottom heat).

2. Wash the sweet potatoes, pat dry and cut into 1 cm wide sticks. Turn the sweet potato sticks in the cornstarch, season with cayenne pepper, salt and pepper. Heat the coconut oil and pour over the sweet potato. Bake in the oven for 15–20 minutes until crispy.

3. Rinse the pollack with cold water, pat dry and cut into small pieces. Whisk the eggs with a little lime zest and juice as well as the curry powder. Mix with the wholegrain spelled flour and the oat flakes to form viscous dough, season well with salt and pepper.

4. Turn the pollack all over in wholemeal spelled flour and pull it through the batter. Fry the saithe in olive oil over medium heat for 2-3 minutes on each side until golden.

5. Finally, mix together all the ingredients for the honey-mustard sauce and season with salt and pepper.

6. Enjoy the sweet potato fries with the baked pollock and the honey-mustard sauce.

VEGGIE FRICADEL WITH MOUNTAIN
CHEESE

INGREDIENTS:

For the meatballs:

1 onion
1 clove of garlic
1 tbsp butter
1 teaspoon smoked
paprika powder 125 ml milk
125 g of oatmeal
1 teaspoon organic mustard
60 g spicy mountain cheese
1 handful of parsley
1 egg salt, pepper
Olive oil for frying

Miscellaneous:

Organic mustard
radish

Approx. 6 meatballs

HOW TO DO IT:

1. Peel the onion and clove of garlic, dice finely and sauté in the butter until translucent. Add the paprika and roast briefly. Top up with the milk, warm up slightly and remove from the stove.

2. Add the oat flakes and mustard to the milk and leave to soak for 15 minutes.

3. In the meantime, grate the mountain cheese finely and chop finely the parsley. Then mix the cheese, parsley and egg with the oat flakes. Season to taste with salt and pepper.

4. Heat the olive oil in a pan. Using an ice cream scoop, add the meatballs to the pan and flatten them a little. Brown the meatballs for about 4 minutes on each side.

5. Enjoy with some mustard and radishes. The vegetarian meatballs taste warm or cold.

WRAPS WITH COD AND PEA CREAM

INGREDIENTS:

For the buckwheat wraps:

150 g buckwheat flour

1 egg, 1 tbsp olive oil

2 tbsp butter

For the pea cream:

1 shallot and 1 clove of garlic each

1 pinch of chili flakes, 1 tbsp olive oil

200 g peas, frozen

70 ml vegetable stock or water

2 tbsp almond butter

For the cod:

200 g cod, boned and skinless
½ organic lime, 1 tbsp olive oil
Miscellaneous:
Baby spinach
Dill, coriander
greens Organic lime
Salt pepper
2 PEOPLE

HOW TO DO IT:

1. Mix the buckwheat flour with 300 ml of water and the egg. Stir in the olive oil and a pinch of salt and leave to soak for 15 minutes. Then gradually bake the wraps in a little butter in a coated pan.

2. In the meantime, peel and slice the shallot and garlic. Sauté together with the chili flakes in olive oil until translucent. Then add the peas and fill up with the vegetable stock. Let the peas simmer over low heat for 3 minutes. Finally, add the almond butter and puree everything very finely. Season to taste with salt and pepper.

3. Rinse the cod with cold water, pat dry and cut into small cubes, season with salt and lime zest. Fry in the olive oil for 2 minutes on each side until translucent.

4. Cover the buckwheat wraps with baby spinach and a little mushy peas, spread the cod over the top and add herbs such as z. B. Sprinkle the dill and coriander. Finally, pour 1 splash of lime juice over it and roll it up tightly.

PULLED LAX BURGER WITH HORSE RADISH YOGURT

INGREDIENTS:

For the Pulled Lax:

250 g salmon fillet, boned and skinless

2 stalks of dill

1 tbsp olive oil

For the horseradish yogurt:

3 tbsp Greek yogurt 10%

½ organic lime

1-2 tbsp freshly grated horseradish
For the cucumber:
½ cucumber
½ organic lime
1 tbsp olive oil
1 handful of dill
Miscellaneous:
2 whole wheat
rolls Baby chard
Salt pepper
2 PEOPLE

HOW TO DO IT:

1. Preheat the oven to 100 ° C circulating air (120 ° C top / bottom heat). Rinse the salmon fillet with cold water and pat dry. Season with a little salt and pepper, cover with the dill stalks and drizzle with the olive oil. Let the salmon steep in the oven for about 15 minutes until translucent. Then carefully tear it into large pieces with 2 forks.

2. In the meantime, stir together the Greek yogurt with a little zest and the juice of the lime. Season to taste with freshly grated horseradish, a little salt and pepper.

3. Turn the cucumber with a spiral cutter into cucumber spaghetti, refine with the olive oil, the juice of the lime and the chopped dill as well as a pinch of salt.

4. For the lax burger, coat the lower half of the whole grain roll with horseradish yoghurt and top with chard salad and pulled lax. Finish with the cucumber spaghetti and the top half of the bun.

ROASTED VEGETABLE SANDWICH
WITH CAPER PESTO

INGREDIENTS:

For the roasted vegetables:

2 peppers, yellow and red

1 zucchini

4 tbsp olive oil, 1 tbsp apple cider vinegar

2 sprigs of rosemary

For the caper pesto:

2 tbsp capers

1 clove of garlic

1 tbsp almond kernels, blanched and roasted

1 handful of parsley

5 tbsp olive oil

2 anchovy fillets in oil, optional

½ lemon

Miscellaneous:

4 slices of wholemeal butter spelled toast

(see p. 92) Rocket, basil

Salt pepper

2 PEOPLE

HOW TO DO IT:

1. Preheat the oven to 220 ° C circulating air (top / bottom heat 240 ° C). Core the peppers and cut into large pieces together with the zucchini. Mix the olive oil with the apple cider vinegar and the finely chopped rosemary. Marinate the vegetables with it.

2. Spread the vegetables on a baking sheet lined with baking paper and season with a little salt and pepper. Roast in the oven for about 10 minutes and then leave to cool.

3. In the meantime, puree the capers together with a peeled clove of garlic, the almond kernels, 1 good handful of parsley and the olive oil to make a pesto. If you like, you can also puree the anchovy fillets. Finally, season to taste with a little lemon juice and pepper.

4. For the sandwich, toast the wholemeal toasted bread until golden, top with a little rocket, the roasted vegetables and, if you like, with pesto. Finally, refine with the plucked basil and finish with another slice of toast.

tip

If you like, you can refine the sandwich with matured pecorino cheese.

SPINACH WAFFLES WITH YOGURT AND CRESS

INGREDIENTS:

For the spinach waffles:
80 g spinach
½ clove of garlic

125 ml milk, also almond milk

1 tbsp olive oil

1 egg

½ tsp pure tartar baking
powder 100–125 g wholemeal
spelled flour 1 squirt of lemon
juice nutmeg

For the lime yogurt:

200 g Greek yogurt

1 organic lime

1 tbsp olive oil

Miscellaneous:

1 tomato

Cress, e.g. B.

Radishcress Salt pepper

Approx. 6 WAFFLES

HOW TO DO IT:

1. Wash the spinach and spin dry. Puree well with the peeled garlic clove, milk and olive oil. Whisk the egg and add.

2. Then mix the baking powder with 100 g wholemeal flour and stir with the spinach milk. If necessary, add a little more flour, so that a viscous dough is formed. Season to taste with a splash of lemon juice, salt, pepper and fresh nutmeg.

3. Let the dough rest for about 10 minutes and then bake in the waffle iron.

4. Mix the yoghurt with the zest and juice of the lime and the olive oil and season with salt and pepper.

5. Garnish the spinach waffles with tomato slices, the lime yoghurt and a little cress.

tip

The waffles also taste very good cold. Mix the lime yoghurt with a little milk to make it creamy, if you like.

PUTELLO TONNATO SANDWICH WITH TURKEY BREAST

INGREDIENTS:

For the turkey breast:

250 g organic turkey breast schnitzel

1 pinch of chili flakes

2 tbsp olive oil

For the tonnato cream:

½ red onion

1 tbsp capers

1 handful of parsley

1 can of tuna, in water

1 tbsp crème fraîche

½ lemon

Miscellaneous:

Whole grain bread, e.g. B. Nut-spelled bread from p. 96 (see also tip p. 39) Romaine lettuce

1 tomato

Salt pepper

2 PEOPLE

HOW TO DO IT:

1. Pound carefully the turkey breast schnitzel flat with a meat tenderizer. Season with a little chili flakes, salt and pepper. Sear in olive oil for 2-3 minutes on each side, then let cool.

2. For the tonnato cream, peel and dice finely the onion, chop finely the capers and parsley. Drain the tuna. Mix everything together well with the tuna and the crème fraîche. Finally, season to taste with a little lemon juice and salt and pepper.

3. For the Putello tonnato sandwich, top the wholemeal bread with a few leaves of romaine lettuce and tomato slices, the turkey breast and tonnato

cream. Finish with another slice of wholemeal bread and press down lightly.

tip

The crème fraîche can also be easily replaced with Greek yogurt (10%).

VEGGIE SLOPPY JOE WITH MOUNTAIN LENS AND CUCUMBER

INGREDIENTS:

For the Sloppy Joe:

1 onion, 2 cloves of garlic
½ chili pepper, 1 red pepper
1 teaspoon mustard seeds, yellow
½ teaspoon cumin, 2 tablespoons
olive oil 100 g mountain lentils
½ teaspoon smoked paprika
1 tbsp whole cane sugar
300 g vegetable broth or water
300 ml cherry tomatoes from the can
1 splash of lime juice

Miscellaneous:

2 whole grain baguette rolls, e.g. rye and buttermilk rolls
from p. 93 Lettuce, 1 cucumber
1 red onion, parsley
Salt pepper
2 PEOPLE

HOW TO DO IT:

1. Peel the onion and the clove of garlic and dice finely as well as the chili and bell pepper. Mortar finely the mustard seeds and cumin and sauté everything in a pan with the olive oil over medium heat until translucent.

2. Then add the mountain lentils, the smoked paprika and the whole cane sugar and roast briefly. Deglaze with the vegetable stock and top up with the cherry tomatoes. Simmer everything together over a low heat for 35–40 minutes until soft. Finally, season to taste with a little lime juice, salt and pepper.

3. Then cut into the wholemeal baguette rolls and fill them with a few leaves of lettuce, cucumber strips and plenty of sloppy. Garnish with a few onion rings and parsley.

tip

The Sloppy Joe is a good alternative to an ordinary Bolognese. Also, tastes great on a baked sweet potato.

COLESLAW BURGER WITH PECAN NUT AND FETA

INGREDIENTS:

For the Coleslaw:

150 g red cabbage

1 red onion

1 carrot (80 g)

1 apple

1 teaspoon mustard seeds, yellow

1 teaspoon caraway seeds

2 tbsp apple cider vinegar

1 tbsp honey

2 tbsp Greek yogurt

2 tbsp tahini

Salt pepper

1 handful of coriander greens

Miscellaneous:

2 whole grain rolls, e.g. rye and buttermilk rolls

Yogurt, lettuce

Feta cheese

1 handful of pecans

2 PEOPLE

HOW TO DO IT:

1. Slice the red cabbage and the peeled red onion into very fine strips. Peel the carrot and grate finely with the apple. Finely mortar the mustard seeds and caraway seeds and mix everything together.

2. Marinate the Coleslaw with the apple cider vinegar, honey, Greek yoghurt and tahini and stir well. Then season with salt and pepper and refine with finely chopped coriander leaves.

3. For the coleslaw burger, coat the whole grain rolls with a little yogurt. Top with lettuce, feta cheese, coleslaw and 1 handful of pecans as desired.

tip

The Coleslaw can of course also be prepared with white cabbage or pointed cabbage.

SWEET PUMPKIN SANDWICH WITH PEANUT JUTS

INGREDIENTS:

For the pumpkin mash:
400 g Hokkaido pumpkin
2 tbsp coconut oil

40 g whole cane sugar

2 organic oranges

3 tbsp apple cider vinegar

1 stick of cinnamon

½ vanilla pod

1 teaspoon ginger zest

salt

Miscellaneous:

8 Wholegrain butter spelled toast (see p. 92)

Peanut butter

Pumpkin seeds

2 PEOPLE

HOW TO DO IT:

1. Halve the pumpkin, remove the seeds and cut into fine cubes. Then sauté the pumpkin cubes in the coconut oil over medium heat. Add the whole cane sugar and let it caramelize slowly.

2. Deglaze with the freshly squeezed orange juice and apple cider vinegar. Add the cinnamon stick and the pulp of the vanilla pod and simmer everything over a low heat for about 20 minutes.

3. Then remove the spices and press everything with a fork or a potato masher to a coarse puree. Finally refine with ginger zest and a pinch of salt.

4. For the sandwich, toast or toast the toast, coat the lower half with peanut butter and, if you like, top with the pumpkin mash and a few pumpkin seeds. Finish with another slice of toast.

tip

The cleaned kernels of the Hokkaido pumpkin can be roasted in the oven and are a great snack.

FRENCH TOAST WITH CHUTNEY AND AVOCADO

INGREDIENTS:

For the tomato chutney:
100 g onions
500 g ripe tomatoes on the vine
1 tbsp olive oil
½ teaspoon coriander seeds
1 bay leaf
1 organic
lemon salt

2–4 tbsp maple syrup
For the French toast:
2 eggs
4 tablespoons of milk
1 pinch of cayenne pepper
8 slices of wholegrain buttered spelled toast (see p. 92)
Miscellaneous:
1 avocado
Coriander or parsley
2 PEOPLE

HOW TO DO IT:

1. For the tomato chutney, cut the onion into fine cubes and the tomatoes into large pieces. Steam the onion cubes in a large saucepan in olive oil, then add the crushed coriander seeds and the bay leaf. Top up with the tomato pieces then add a little zest, the juice of the lemon and a pinch of salt.

2. Mix with 2 tablespoons of maple syrup and reduce to a creamy consistency over a low heat for about 20 minutes. Finally, season to taste with the rest of the maple syrup.

3. For the French toast, whisk the eggs with the milk and season with cayenne pepper and a little salt. Soak the slices of toast bit by bit in the egg mixture from both sides.

4. Halve the avocado, remove the core, remove from the skin and cut into fine slices. Top each slice of toast with avocado and the tomato chutney as desired. Refine with some freshly plucked herbs and finish with a second slice of toast. Lightly press.

5. Fry the French toast on both sides over medium heat in a non-stick pan until golden.

tip

The tomato chutney becomes even fruity if you add a grated apple while it is cooking.

WHOLE GRAIN BUTTER SPELLED TOAST BREAD

INGREDIENTS:

10 g fresh yeast
10 g whole cane sugar
5 g salt
300 g wholemeal spelled flour
30 g butter or coconut oil
1 TOAST BREAD

HOW TO DO IT:

1. Mix 220 ml of lukewarm water with the yeast, whole cane sugar and salt. Add the flour and mix all ingredients briefly on the lowest setting of the food processor. Then work on the second stage for about 10 minutes to form elastic and smooth dough.

2. Cover and let the dough rise in a warm place for about 1 hour and then place it on a floured work surface. Let rest for 10 minutes.

3. Shape a strand about 20 cm long and divide it into four equal pieces. To do this, halve the dough once and halve the resulting halves as well.

4. Grease a 500 g toast baking pan or a 20 cm loaf pan well and place the dough pieces in the greased pan, turned by 90 degrees, that is, diagonally next to each other. Let rise for another 45 minutes. Preheat the oven to 200 ° C fan oven (210 ° C top / bottom heat).

5. Bake the bread until golden for 30-40 minutes, then immediately remove it from the tin and let it cool down.

RYE BUTTERMILK BUNS

INGREDIENTS:

220 ml buttermilk, room temperature
20 g fresh yeast
5 g whole cane sugar
5 g salt
1 tbsp apple cider vinegar
100 g whole wheat flour
150 g whole grain rye flour
4–6 ROLLS

HOW TO DO IT:

1. Mix the buttermilk with the yeast, whole cane sugar, salt and apple

vinegar. Add the flour and mix all ingredients briefly on the lowest setting of the food processor, then work on the second setting for about 5 minutes to form elastic and smooth dough.

2. Cover and let the dough rise in a warm place for about 1 hour. Then work the dough on a floured work surface and let it rest for 10 minutes.

3. Shape it into a strand and divide it into four or six equal pieces, depending on your preference. These look round again and spread out on a baking sheet lined with baking paper. Let the rolls rise for another 30–40 minutes.

4. In the meantime, preheat the oven to 200 ° C (210 ° C top / bottom heat) and place an ovenproof dish filled with water on the bottom of the oven. Bake the rolls for 12–15 minutes and then leave to cool.

tip

If you like, you can incorporate kernels and nuts into the dough or refine the rolls "on top". To do this, brush the rolls with a little water before baking and sprinkle with the kernels or nuts.

BENTO WITH NUT BREAD AND PEANUT JUTS

INGREDIENTS:

For the nut-spelled bread:
500 g wholemeal spelled flour
1 packet of dry yeast
2 tbsp apple cider vinegar
1 tbsp olive oil
2 teaspoons of salt
60 g dried berries
60 g hazelnut kernels
Miscellaneous:
Peanut butter
Romaine lettuce
Cucumber

Cherry tomatoes
Apple
½ lemon
2 PEOPLE

HOW TO DO IT:

1. Mix the wholemeal spelled flour with the dry yeast. Knead together with the apple cider vinegar, 300 ml water, olive oil and salt to form dough. Finally, work in the dried berries and coarsely chopped hazelnuts.

2. Cover the dough and let it rest in a warm place for half an hour. Then knead again and put in a greased loaf pan. Let rise for another 30 minutes.

3. In the meantime, preheat the oven to 180 ° C (200 ° C top / bottom heat) and bake the bread for 30–45 minutes. Let cool slightly and fall out of the mold.

4. Fill the bento box with peanut butter. Wrap romaine lettuce, cucumber slices and cherry tomatoes. In addition, cut 1 apple into slices and marinate with a splash of lemon juice.

tip

The bread is ready when it sounds "hollow" when you tap it lightly. It can be varied as you wish: Simply work in 1 handful of olives instead of the dried berries.

TACO-BENTO WITH CHILI CHICKEN AND GUACAMOLE

INGREDIENTS:

For the tacos:
250 g wholemeal spelled flour
1 tbsp coconut oil
1 teaspoon turmeric
Coconut oil for frying
For the chili chicken:
300 g chicken breast

1 lime
2 tbsp olive oil
2 tbsp tamari soy sauce
1 chili pepper
Miscellaneous:
1 tomato and 1 pepper each
1 red onion spring onion
Coriander green
salad
Guacamole
Salt pepper
2 PEOPLE

HOW TO DO IT:

1. Firstly, knead the whole-grain spelled flour with liquid coconut oil, turmeric, 1 teaspoon of salt and 150–170 ml of water to form smooth dough. Cover and let it rest for 20 minutes. Then halve the dough and cut the halves into eighths. Roll out the dough pieces thinly on a floured surface and bake on both sides in a hot pan.

2. Cut the chicken breast into small pieces and marinate for 20 minutes with the juice of the lime, olive oil, soy sauce and a finely chopped chili pepper.

3. Sear the chicken breast pieces in a pan for 3–5 minutes on each side and season with salt and pepper to taste.

4. For the bento box, cut the vegetables into small pieces, pack some lettuce leaves and the guacamole. Cover the tacos fresh as you like and enjoy.

tip

The chicken breast becomes even more aromatic if you let it steep in the marinade overnight.

SUMMERROLLS BENTO WITH MANGO CUCUMBER SALAD

INGREDIENTS:

For the summer rolls:
1 avocado and 1 paprika each
1 carrot, romaine lettuce
Rice paper
1 handful each of Thai basil and mint
150 g polar sea prawns

For the peanut sauce:

150 g peanut butter

2–3 tablespoons tamari soy sauce

1 teaspoon ginger zest, ½ chili pepper

For the mango and cucumber salad:

1 ripe mango and 1 cucumber each

1 chili pepper

2 stalks of spring onions

3 tbsp sesame oil

1 tbsp brown rice vinegar

1 handful of coriander greens

1 handful of peanuts

Salt pepper

2 PEOPLE

HOW TO DO IT:

1. Firstly, cut the avocado in half, remove the stone and remove the pulp from the skin. Cut into thin slices. Core the peppers, peel the carrot and cut into fine strips with the romaine lettuce.

2. For the summer rolls, moisten gradually the rice paper in warm water until it becomes elastic. Top with freshly plucked herbs, sea prawns, vegetables and avocado as desired. Make sure that the rolls do not get too full and that they can be rolled up easily.

3. For the sauce, mix the peanut butter with the soy sauce, season with freshly grated ginger and finely chopped chili pepper and stir creamy with a little water.

4. For the salad, peel the mango, remove the stone and cut the pulp and the cucumber into cubes. Cut the pepper and spring onion into fine rings and mix everything with the sesame oil and brown rice vinegar. Finally, season with a little salt and pepper and refine with chopped coriander greens and peanuts

Tips

If you want to do without the rice paper, you can also wrap the summer rolls directly in a lettuce leaf.

The rolls can be prepared the day before and stored airtight in the refrigerator. A leaf of lettuce between the rolls prevents them from sticking together.

FALAFEL-BENTO WITH HUMMUS AND SALAD

INGREDIENTS:
For the falafel balls:
200 g chickpeas, dried
100 g onions
1 clove of garlic

1 handful of basil

1 teaspoon cumin

Olive oil for frying

For the hummus:

400 g chickpeas, canned (250 g drained weight)

1 clove of garlic, 2 tbsp tahini

2 tbsp olive oil, ½ lemon

1 pinch of cumin

For the tomato and cucumber salad:

200 g cherry tomatoes

2 small cucumbers, 1 pepper

1 handful of Thai basil

4 tbsp sesame oil, ½ lemon

Salt pepper

2 PEOPLE

HOW TO DO IT:

1. Soak the chickpeas in plenty of water overnight and then drain well. Peel and chop roughly the onion and clove of garlic. Pluck the basil leaves from the stems. Puree everything together in the chopper and season to taste with salt, pepper and the cumin.

2. Now shape even balls - if you like, use an ice cream scoop - and fry them in a pan over medium heat with a little olive oil on both sides until golden.

3. For the hummus, drain the chickpeas and peel the garlic clove. Puree together with the tahini, olive oil and 2-5 tablespoons of water until the mixture becomes creamy. Season to taste with a little zest and juice of the lemon, salt and pepper and the cumin.

4. For the salad, cut the cherry tomatoes in half and cut the cucumber lengthways into fine slices with a peeler. Chop the pepper and the Thai basil and season with sesame oil, a little lemon juice, salt and pepper.

tip

The falafel balls and hummus can be prepared the day before and can be kept in the refrigerator for a few days.

SATÉ-BENTO WITH CURRY SAUCE AND NATURAL RICE SALAD

INGREDIENTS:

For the satay skewers:

300 g chicken breast

6 tbsp tamari soy sauce

1 tbsp whole cane sugar

1 organic lime and 1 chili pepper each

2 tbsp coconut oil
For the curry sauce:
150 g almond butter
2–4 tbsp coconut milk
2 tsp Madras curry powder
Chili pepper, to taste
For the brown rice salad:
60 g brown rice
½ mango, 1 bell pepper
1 red onion and 1 chili pepper each
2 tbsp sesame oil, ½ lime
1 handful of coriander greens
Coconut flakes
Salt pepper
2 PEOPLE

HOW TO DO IT:

1. For the satay skewers, cut the chicken breast lengthways into strips. Marinate for at least half an hour in soy sauce, whole cane sugar, zest and juice of the lime and chopped chili pepper. Then skewer and fry in coconut oil over medium heat for about 3 minutes per side.

2. For the sauce, mix the almond butter with the coconut milk, the curry powder and some finely chopped chili pepper. Season to taste with salt and pepper.

3. Rinse the brown rice with cold water and cook in 150 ml water for about 30 minutes, then let it cool.

4. In the meantime, cut the mango, bell peppers and red onion into small cubes. Chop finely the chili pepper. Add everything to the boiled rice and marinate with the sesame oil and the juice of the lime. Season to taste with salt and pepper and refine with finely chopped coriander greens and coconut flakes.

tip

Matching edamame is available in the Asia store. Simply blanch briefly in salted water and then sprinkle with a little sea salt.

ANTIPASTI-BENTO WITH QUINOA SALAD AND OLIVES

INGREDIENTS:
For the antipasti:
1 zucchini and 1 paprika each
200 g mushrooms
2 sprigs of rosemary

1 clove of garlic, 4 tablespoons of olive oil

2 tbsp light balsamic vinegar

1 handful of pine nuts, toasted

1 handful of basil

Olive oil for frying

For the quinoa salad:

125 g quinoa

250 ml vegetable stock or water

2 tomatoes

1 handful of Kalamata olives, pitted

1 handful of rocket, 3 tablespoons of olive oil

1 tbsp light balsamic vinegar

For the tomato mozzarella:

1 scoop of mozzarella

1 ripe vine tomato

some basil, 1 tbsp olive oil

Salt pepper

2 PEOPLE

HOW TO DO IT:

1. Firstly, cut the antipasti vegetables into bite-sized pieces, chop finely the rosemary and peeled garlic. Fry gradually the vegetables in a little olive oil, refine with a little rosemary and garlic shortly before the end. Then marinate with 4 tablespoons of olive oil and the light balsamic vinegar, season with salt and pepper. Refine with roasted pine nuts and finely chopped basil.

2. Rinse the quinoa well under cold water. Bring the vegetable stock to the boil with a little salt, add the quinoa and cover and simmer over a low heat for about 15 minutes. Then let it cool down. Dice finely the tomatoes and fold them into the quinoa together with the Kalamata olives and some rocket. Finally, marinate with the olive oil and light balsamic vinegar. Season to taste with a little salt and pepper.

3. Cut the mozzarella and tomato into slices and layer them alternately, season with salt and pepper and refine with a little finely chopped basil and olive oil.

tip

The antipasti tastes even more aromatic the next day, ideally warm to room temperature before consumption.

VEGETABLE BOX WITH SHEEP CHEESE QUARK

INGREDIENTS:

For the vegetable box:

500 g vegetables, e.g. B. carrots, celery, peppers, radishes, kohlrabi, vine tomatoes

For the sheep cheese curd:

100 g sheep cheese

150 g quark

1 tbsp olive oil

2 stalks of spring onions

½ clove of garlic

1 handful of parsley

about 10 leaves of mint

1-2 tbsp milk or water

Salt pepper

2 PEOPLE

HOW TO DO IT:

1. Wash and peel the vegetables well. Pull the strings on the celery. Then cut everything into fine sticks.

2. Crumble finely the sheep's cheese and stir together with the quark and olive oil. Cut the spring onion and the peeled garlic into fine slices and add to the quark together with the herbs. Puree everything together finely and mix with a little milk or water until creamy. Finally, just add salt and pepper to taste.

tip

The vegetables can be wrapped in a damp cloth in the refrigerator and stored overnight.

FRUIT BOX WITH MATCHA YOGURT AND BASIL

INGREDIENTS:

For the fruit box:

500 g seasonal fruit, e.g. B. apples, pears, apricots, kiwi, grapefruit, grapes, mango, physalis

1 handful of pomegranate seeds

1 handful of basil

1 orange

1 tbsp hazelnut oil

1 tbsp honey, optional

For the matcha yogurt:

150 g Greek yogurt

½ vanilla pod

1 organic lime

1 teaspoon honey

1-2 teaspoons of matcha

1 handful of almond kernels, toasted

2 PEOPLE

HOW TO DO IT:

1. Depending on the type and fruit, wash, peel and cut the fruit into small pieces. Mix with the pomegranate seeds and finely chopped basil. Marinate with the juice of the orange and the hazelnut oil and sweeten with a little honey.

2. Mix the Greek yogurt with the pulp of the vanilla pod, a little zest and juice of the lime and a little honey until creamy. Stir in 1–2 teaspoons of matcha, depending on the desired intensity. Finally, refine with almond kernels.

tip

Can be easily prepared the day before and is the perfect vitamin bomb for in between.

SPICY VEGETABLE CHIPS WITH SESAME AND ROSEMARY

INGREDIENTS:

500 g vegetables, e.g. B. beetroot, sweet potatoes, carrots, parsnips, kale

1-2 tablespoons of extra virgin olive
oil Sesame seeds
rosemary
Salt pepper
2 PEOPLE

HOW TO DO IT:

1. Wash the vegetables well and pat dry. Cut the vegetables into fine slices with a vegetable slicer. Remove the thick, hard stalk from the kale.

2. Marinate the vegetables with olive oil, a pinch of salt and pepper. Stir in sesame seeds or chopped rosemary to taste.

3. Spread the vegetable slices on a baking tray lined with baking paper and dry in the oven at around 120 ° C for 30–60 minutes. The baking time varies depending on the type of vegetable and the thickness of the slices. Use a kitchen towel to leave the oven door ajar so that the moisture can escape. It is best to turn the vegetables halfway through.

4. The chips should be kept as airtight as possible.

Tips

Place the vegetables close together on the tray, as they will shrink a lot during baking. The chips can be made from almost any type of vegetable. The marinade can also be changed to taste with other herbs and spices.

CURRY POPCORN WITH HONEY
AND SEA SALT

INGREDIENTS:

For the popcorn:
1-2 tbsp coconut oil
75 g popcorn corn
For the marinade:
2 tbsp cocoa butter or coconut oil
2 tbsp honey
1 tbsp Madras curry powder

1 teaspoon sea salt

2 PEOPLE

HOW TO DO IT:

1. For the popcorn, put the coconut oil in a large saucepan so that the base is evenly covered and heat it up. Add the corn and close with a lid on medium heat for 4-5 minutes. Shake the pot back and forth in between, keeping the lid closed. If you can no longer hear any noises, remove the pan from the stove.

2. Then heat the cocoa butter and stir in the curry powder and honey. Use it to marinate the popcorn and sprinkle with a little sea salt.

Tips

Keep the curry popcorn airtight. There are countless variations of curry: It is worth trying your way through the different types.

CHERRY POWERBALLS WITH COCOA NIBS

INGREDIENTS:

80 g blanched almonds
40 g cashew nuts
120 g dried cherries
60 g dates
½ organic lime
½ vanilla
pod salt
Cocoa nibs to roll over

Approx. 20 POWERBALLS

HOW TO DO IT:

1. Chop finely the almonds with the cashew nuts in a food processor. Add the cherries and dates and mix briefly. Then add the zest and juice of half a lime, the pulp of the vanilla pod and a pinch of salt. Mix everything together until you get a tough measure.

2. Shape the cherry mixture into a roll and cut into pieces of equal size, then shape them into balls.

3. Finally, chop finely the cocoa nibs and roll the Powerballs in them all around.

tip

The Powerballs taste best when slightly chilled.

NUT POWER BAR WITH HONEY AND CHIA SEEDS

INGREDIENTS:

160 g nuts, e.g. B. almonds, cashew nuts, pecans, pistachios, pumpkin seeds
100 g dried fruits, e.g. B. cranberries, cherries, physalis
60 g oatmeal
1 tbsp sesame seeds
1 tbsp chia seeds
1 tbsp coconut oil
50 g honey
50 g raw cane sugar
Approx. 8 BARS

HOW TO DO IT:

1. Roughly chop the nuts and cut the dried fruit into small pieces. Mix both with oatmeal, sesame seeds and chia seeds.

2. Warm the coconut oil with the honey and stir in the raw cane sugar. Then mix well with the nut mixture.

3. Preheat the oven to 160 ° C fan oven. Line a baking dish (approx. 18 x 18 cm) with baking paper and distribute the nut mixture evenly on it. Using a second baking paper, press the tough mixture very firmly into the mold and bake for about 30 minutes until golden.

4. Cut eight power bars from it while still lukewarm and let cool down completely.

WAFFLES WITH BLUEBERRIES AND COCOA NIBS

INGREDIENTS:

2 eggs

80 g coconut blossom sugar

1 pinch of cinnamon powder

½ vanilla pod 30 g

coconut oil 1

organic orange 150

ml almond milk

200 g whole wheat or spelled flour

1 tsp pure tartar baking powder

100 g blueberries

2 tbsp cocoa nibs

Approx. 6 WAFFLES

HOW TO DO IT:

1. First, whip the eggs with the coconut blossom sugar, cinnamon and the pulp of the vanilla pod until creamy.

2. In the meantime, melt the coconut oil, add the zest and juice of the orange and fill up with the almond milk.

3. Mix the whole wheat flour with the tartar baking powder and carefully stir into the almond milk. Finally, fold in the beaten eggs and add the blueberries and cocoa nibs.

4. Preheat the waffle iron and grease a little. Gradually fry the waffles until golden. Then let cool on a rack. A delicious snack on the go!

CPSIA information can be obtained
at www.ICGtesting.com
Printed in the USA
BVHW011649210621
610124BV00013B/2707

9 781802 321777